Understanding Boilerplate

A Riveting Guide to
Common Contract
Clauses

Ethan Mobley

Table of Contents

Introduction

If you are reading this book, you probably encounter contracts in your work or business and hope to gain a better understanding of common contractual language. You are probably also in the minority of people that closely read contracts and actually care to understand everything in those contracts. For that, you should be proud. Understanding legal language commonly found in contracts will make you more competitive in the workplace and sure-footed in your personal life. After all, knowledge is power!

This book is written for anybody that has ever wondered what "indemnification" means and is specifically geared towards non-legal professionals. As such, this book will make generalizations with respect to contract law and interpretation. It will simplify overly verbose legal language (often called "legalese") into basic English. In so doing, it is important to realize some nuance may be lost, but at that expense you will gain a working knowledge of important contractual provisions. As such, please keep in mind that nothing contained in this book should be construed as legal advice; if you need legal advice, please consult a licensed attorney.

Contracts set forth the agreed upon terms and conditions with respect to a specific subject matter. Whether it is a contract for the sale of property or a software license agreement, well-drafted contracts also invariably contain "boilerplate" clauses. Boilerplate is typically found at the end of a contract, and generally speaking, sets forth common (and usually, rather boring) provisions that are independent from the subject matter of the agreement. Boilerplate is in contrast to *subject matter* clauses that do the real work capturing the meaning of the parties in the agreement. In our software license example, the terms relating to the license grant and payment would be what we call "subject matter" clauses, because they describe particulars relating to the software itself; a clause stating the agreement will be governed by California law would be considered boilerplate because it is unrelated to the software.

In the legal world, boilerplate is as important as it is mundane. Anyone who has read a legal agreement has encountered these "boilerplate" provisions of the document that seem to either state the obvious, or simply not say anything at all. To the trained mind, however, boilerplate serves a meaningful purpose that compliments the overall agreement.

For each boilerplate clause discussed, this book will take a formulaic approach. First, we will look at several sample clauses based on type. Second, this book will translate the overall meaning as simply as possible. Third, we will discuss the general importance of each boilerplate clause. The clauses are organized alphabetically as follows:

Clauses

Assignment

> **Example 1**: "Neither this Agreement nor any interests or obligations granted hereunder may be assigned, in whole or in part, or transferred, by operation of law or otherwise, to any third party, unless the non-assigning party gives prior written consent."

> **Example 2**: "Neither party to this Agreement shall assign or otherwise transfer its rights or obligations under this Agreement to any third party, except to a parent, subsidiary, or affiliate, without the other party's prior written consent."

Assignment clauses typically prevent or limit the ability to transfer an agreement to a third party. In Example 1 above, the clause prevents the contract from being transferred to a third party without permission of the non-transferring party. Example 2 also restricts assignment to unrelated third parties, but allows the contract to be transferred to related companies without permission. Both examples are common in the business world and are used in different contexts. Example 1 may be used when a contract really needs to be performed by a particular entity; example 2 is common where one of the contracting parties (the potential assignee) has a layered or multi-level corporate structure and it would be reasonable to allow a contract to be transferred within a family of companies. Assignment clauses are important because most contracts can be assigned freely to another party unless an assignment clause limits the parties' ability to do so.

Attorneys' Fees

> **Example 1**: "In the event of a dispute between the parties concerning the terms and provisions of this Agreement, the party prevailing in the dispute shall be entitled to collect from the other party all costs incurred in such dispute, including reasonable attorneys' fees."

Example 2: "In the event either party institutes an action or proceeding against the other party with regard to this Assignment, the prevailing party of such action shall be entitled to recover from the non-prevailing party its attorneys' fees and costs incurred in such action or proceeding, in addition to all other remedies provided by law."

Attorneys' fees clauses shift the burden of paying for attorneys in a dispute from one party to another. In the United States, parties to a dispute are usually responsible for paying for their own attorneys' fees and costs – even if they are not at fault or are successful in the dispute. Attorneys' fees clauses, such as Examples 1 and 2 above, shift the cost of paying for *both* sides' attorneys to the losing party. Much of the world presumptively requires the losing party to pay all attorneys' fees, but the United States does not follow this rule; as such, attorneys' fee clauses are often seen as making the cost of enforcing an agreement more fair and disincentivizes bringing meritless lawsuits.

Choice of Law

Example 1: "This Agreement shall be governed by and construed in accordance with the substantive laws of the State of Minnesota without regard to the choice of law principles thereof."

Example 2: "This Agreement shall be governed by the laws of the State of California, regardless of choice of law principles, as to all matters, including but not limited to matters of validity, construction, effect, performance and remedies."

In contracts, unlike or areas of law, parties generally get to decide which jurisdiction's laws apply to the interpretation of their contract. Contracts often take advantage of this and state which jurisdiction's laws apply using a Choice of Law clause. These clauses are typically straightforward with the exception of references to "choice of law principles." The language, "without regard to choice of law principles," avoids a possible scenario where the chosen jurisdiction has procedural laws that would change the controlling jurisdiction to some other jurisdiction. Key to this unlikely situation is the difference between "substantive" and "procedural" laws, but that is beyond the scope of this book. For now, just understand the phrase, "without regard to choice of law principles," helps ensure the contract is actually interpreted by the intended jurisdiction.

Counterparts

> **Example 1**: "This Agreement may be executed in more than one counterpart, each of which shall be deemed to be an original, but all of which together shall constitute one and the same instrument."

> **Example 2**: "This Agreement may be executed in separate counterparts, any one of which need not contain signatures of more than one party, but all of which when taken together constitute one and the same Agreement."

Counterparts clauses are premised on the understanding that signors may not be able to conveniently sign the same original copy of an agreement. Instead, counterparts clauses allow parties to sign different copies and recognize that signatures on separate documents can be treated as being on the same document. As such, signors need not be in the same place to sign a document, nor do they need to wait for a physical copy signed by the other party before they can execute the agreement. These clauses are generally quite convenient for all involved and are very common in today's global economy.

Dispute Resolution

Example 1: "Subject to the Contractor's right to seek injunctive relief in court, any dispute or claim arising out of or in relation to or connection to this Agreement, including any dispute as to the construction, validity, interpretation, enforceability or breach of this Agreement, shall be settled by arbitration administered by the American Arbitration Association and judgment upon the award rendered by the arbitrator(s) may be entered in any court having jurisdiction thereof."

Example 2: "Any and all claims and disputes arising under or relating to this Agreement shall be settled by binding arbitration in the state of Georgia or another location mutually agreeable to the parties. An award of arbitration may be confirmed in a court of competent jurisdiction."

Arbitration clauses mandate that any dispute arising from a contract be settled by an arbitrator rather than the courts. These clauses may specify a particular type of arbitration and rules (e.g. arbitration by the American Arbitration Association as in Example 1) or the clause may allow the parties to decide on the arbitration rules at a later date (e.g. as mutually agreed upon in Example 2). These clauses also tend to specify where the arbitration will occur ("venue") and may also specify the governing law that the arbitrator would apply to the dispute. Without an arbitration clause, disputes may be handled by federal or state courts. Use of arbitration is sometimes preferred by businesses because arbitration is often more cost-effective than using the courts; but for consumers, arbitration clauses can make it more difficult to enforce an agreement against a business and often is not desirable.

Entire Agreement

Example 1: "This Agreement constitutes the entire agreement between the Parties with respect to the subject matter of this Agreement and supersedes all prior agreements, understandings and negotiations, whether written or oral, between the parties."

Example 2: "This Agreement constitutes the entire agreement between the parties hereto with respect to the matters herein contained, and all prior discussions and agreements with respect thereto, except to the extent set forth in this Agreement, shall be of no further force and effect."

Entire agreement clauses ensure that negotiated terms leading up to a contract are only included if actually written in the final contract. These clauses provide certainty for both parties, because they ensure that if any promises were made (or terms discussed) prior to the contract, they are not enforceable unless written in the signed contract. Without this type of clause, disputes can arise disputes over whether informal discussions or negotiations leading up to a contract are enforceable as a term of the final contract – even if not actually written in the contract.

Some variations of this clause, such as in Example 1, also include the term "superseding" (or similar). Superseding language comes into play when the parties previously signed a contract on a particular subject and now want to replace the older contract with a new contract. In that case, the superseding language in Example 1 means the newer contract replaces the old contract and the old contract is no longer relevant for the particular subject at hand.

Force Majeure

Example 1: "In the event either party is unable to perform its obligations under the terms of this Agreement because of acts of God, strike, war, embargo, or damage that is reasonably beyond its control, or any other cause that is reasonably beyond its control, such party shall not be liable for damages to the other or for any damages resulting from such failure to perform or otherwise from such causes."

Example 2: "Neither Party shall lose any rights hereunder or be liable to the other party for damages or losses due to lack of performance by the defaulting party if the failure is caused by war, strike, fire, Acts of God, earthquake, flood, embargo, governmental acts or orders or restrictions, or any other reason where failure to perform is beyond the reasonable control and not caused by the negligence or intentional conduct of the non-performing party, and such party has exerted all reasonable efforts to avoid or remedy such force majeure."

Force majeure clauses allow parties to get out of a contract in the event there is some unforeseeable, large scale event. Typically, these "force majeure events" are listed as including certain natural disasters, war, and other geopolitical strife that was not foreseeable at the time the contract was made. If a force majeure clause is included in a contract and a force majeure event occurs, the parties generally are not bound to continue performing under the contract. As such, force majeure clauses act as a form of quasi-insurance for both parties by reducing risk if something totally unpredictable happens in the world that affects their contract.

Headings

Example 1: "The headings in this Agreement are for convenience only and shall not limit or otherwise affect the meaning of this Agreement."

Example 2: "The headings of sections are solely for convenience of reference and shall not affect the meaning hereof."

The headings clause is classic boilerplate. Quite simply, it means that the words in any headings appearing in an agreement don't influence the meaning of the agreement. It may seem difficult to imagine how headings *would* affect the agreement's meaning, but it is possible if the headings are poorly written. To cover bases, headings clauses are used so that just in case a heading is confusing and poorly written, it doesn't cause the agreement to be interpreted in an unintended way.

Indemnification

Example 1: "The Contractor shall indemnify and hold the Company, its officers, boards, employees and agents harmless from any and all claims, injuries, suits, actions, judgments, damages, losses, costs, expenses and liabilities of any kind whatsoever, including but not limited to, attorney's fees and costs of defense which may be the result of willful, negligent or tortious conducts arising out of the Contractor's performance of this Agreement, regardless of whether or not the negligent act is caused in part by the Company."

Example 2: "Developer shall indemnify, defend and hold harmless Company against any "Indemnified Claim," meaning all liabilities, claims, suits, proceedings, and costs (including reasonable attorney fees) arising from: (i) Developer's negligence or willful misconduct in connection with its provision of Services under this Agreement; (ii) Developer's material violation of any term of this Agreement; (iii) Developer's violation of any third-party right, including without limitation any privacy or intellectual property rights; (iv) Developer's violation of any applicable law, rule, or regulation; (v) any third-party claim alleging that Developer's Product infringes a third party's copyright, trademark, patent, or trade secret right."

Indemnification clauses are an extremely common way to transfer risk from one party to another. Risk is transferred by specifying that one party will reimburse (i.e. "indemnify") the other party for certain damages as a result of their actions. Indemnification clauses can sometimes shift risk unfairly, so it is important to pay close attention to these clauses when you see them in contracts.

Indemnification clauses can take many forms but all follow a basic pattern. One party (the "Indemnitor") indemnifies the other party (the "Indemnitee") for certain actions pertaining to the performance of an agreement. In other words, the Indemnitor will reimburse the Indemnitee for the Indemnitor's bad actions in the course of performing the agreement. Reimbursement usually includes any damages, attorneys' fees, and costs associated with the indemnitors bad actions. Bad actions can be spelled out (as in Example 2) or more generically described (as in Example 1).

Importantly, some indemnification clauses are more "fair" than others. Take Example 1 above – here, the Indemnitor can be forced to reimburse the Indemnitee, even if the Indemnitee was also at fault; the operative language in this case is, "whether or not the negligent act is caused in part by the [Indemnitee]." Indemnification clauses like Example 1 can leave Indemnitors reimbursing Indemnitees for more than their fair share but are quite common. By contrast, Example 2 only requires the Indemnitor to reimburse the Indemnitee if the Indemnitor was completely to blame for the damages. Given the wide range of risk shifting that indemnification clauses can effectuate, it is important to understand exactly (1) what circumstances trigger the shifting of financial responsibility; (2) who agrees to take financial responsibility under these conditions; and (3) how much is at stake in the event a situation that triggers liability arises.

Independent Contractor

Example 1: "The Parties are independent contractors and this Agreement shall not create any form of partnership, joint venture, agency or employment relationship between the Parties."

Example 2: "Each Party shall act solely as an independent contractor. Nothing in this Agreement shall be construed to give either Party the power or authority to bind the other Party in any way, and neither party shall hold itself out as an agent or partner of the other party. Nothing herein shall be construed to create the relationship of partners, principal and agent, or joint-venture partners between the Parties."

Independent contractor clauses are intended to memorialize that both parties are distinctly independent of each other. Put differently, independent contractor clauses are intended to reduce the likelihood a court would find the parties to be "partners," "agents," or "joint venturers." When parties are partners, agents, or joint venturers, the parties incur greater legal risk, because each party can generally be held accountable for the actions of the other party. As such, businesses in particular often disclaim "partners," "agents," or "joint venture" status as a way to reduce liability for actions from the other party to a contract.

Limitation of Liability

Example 1: "In no event shall the Company be liable for any direct, indirect, special, incidental, consequential, reliance or exemplary damages including, but not limited to, loss of profits, loss of data or loss of use damages, even if the Company has been advised of the possibility of the same. Some jurisdictions do not allow the exclusion of certain warranties or the limitation or exclusion of liability for incidental or consequential damages, so some of the above limitations may not apply to You. In not event, however, shall the maximum liability of the Company arising out of or in connection with this Agreement, whether in contract, tort, or otherwise, exceed the greater of: (i) the fees You paid to the Company for the Product, or (ii) five thousand dollars ($5,000)."

Example 2: "In no event shall Company be liable to Agent or any third party for any damages, whether in any action of contract or tort, for loss of profits, loss of use, business losses, or any other indirect, incidental, special, punitive or consequential damages which may arise in connection with this Agreement or the services provided hereunder, each of which is hereby precluded and waived by agreement of the parties, even if Company has been advised of the possibility of such damages. In no event shall Company's aggregate and cumulative liability for damages hereunder exceed the lesser of (a) $50,000, or (b) the amount of compensation paid to Agent under this Agreement for the three month period prior to the event giving rise to damages."

Limitation of liability clauses create a cap on the amount of damages one party could be held liable for under the agreement. Often, businesses selling products or services will use limitation of liability clauses to reduce their risk associated with a sale, service, or transaction. A limitation of liability clause will always list a monetary value or a formula for calculating the maximum liability under the agreement. Examples 1 and 2 contain both dollar values and formulas to calculate the cap. These clauses are useful for limiting risk associated with an agreement in a predictable way, but should be examined closely, as they can dramatically reduce one party's ability to recover appropriate damages if there is a dispute.

Modification

> **Example 1**: "This Agreement shall not be modified except as mutually agreed upon in writing signed by both parties."

> **Example 2**: "This Agreement may not be modified or amended except pursuant to a written instrument executed by both parties."

Agreements are supposed to capture the intent of parties at the time of the agreement. However, sometimes circumstances change or mistakes were made in the original agreement that the parties wish to change. Recognizing that things may change, contracts often include a modification clause to control the process by which it can be amended.

Typically, modification clauses state an agreement cannot be modified unless both parties agree to do so in writing; this clause removes all doubt that a contract could potentially be modified verbally, and instead requires both parties to agree (often with signature) to any changes in writing. As a result, this clause ensures that all terms in a contract are written down, and neither party can try to claim a contract was modified in their favor down the road, unless evidenced in writing with signatures of both parties.

Notice

Example 1: "Written notices to Company required to be sent under this Agreement shall be sent to the address set forth below."

Example 2: "Any notice, request, instruction or other document that may be given hereunder by any party to the other shall be in writing and will be deemed to have been duly given (a) on the date of delivery if delivered electronically, or (b) on the second business day following the date of dispatch if delivered by a reputable next day courier service. All notices hereunder shall be delivered to the addresses in the signature block for each respective party."

Notice clauses provide contact information for anything relating to the contract, such as a physical addresses for each party in Example 1. A notice clause may also provide instruction on *when* a particular notice is deemed effective, which is important in some contracts that condition obligations or duties upon notice being given to the other party.

For example, a data protection agreement may mandate a party notify the other party within forty-eight (48) hours if there has been a data breach. In that case, the notice clause would likely specify how acceptable notice of the breach is given (e.g. email or physical mail) and when the notice is effective (either when notice is *sent* or *received*), which can be important when approaching the 48-hour deadline in our example.

Severability

Example 1: "In the event that any provision of this Agreement shall for any reason be held invalid, illegal or unenforceable in any respect by a court of competent jurisdiction, to such extent such provision shall be deemed null and void and severed from this Agreement, and the remainder hereof shall remain in full force and effect as if the severed provision had never existed."

Example 2: "If any provision in this Agreement shall be held illegal, invalid, or unenforceable in any jurisdiction, said provision shall, as to such jurisdiction be ineffective to the extent of such invalidity, illegality or unenforceability without affecting the validity, legality and enforceability of the remaining provisions. The invalidity of a specific provision in a particular jurisdiction shall not invalidate such provision in any other jurisdiction."

Severability clauses are common in contracts that may be used in numerous jurisdictions and act as a form of insurance if courts find a particular part of the contract unenforceable. These clauses ensure that if any particular part of a contract is unenforceable (i.e. illegal, unlawful, or against public policy as determined by a court), the remaining portions of the contract are still valid and enforceable. Without a severability clause, a contract with many provisions could be completely worthless if even a single, small part is unenforceable. Since enforceability of certain clauses can vary between states or countries, severability clauses serve an important purpose by allowing use of the contract in many jurisdictions without needing to tailor it to the nuances of each jurisdiction's laws.

Survival

Example 1: "Sections 8, 9 and 10 shall survive termination of this Agreement."

Example 2: "The confidentiality provisions contained in this Agreement shall survive termination of this Agreement for a period of three (3) years."

Survival clauses work in conjunction with "term" clauses that exist in most Contracts. Term clauses specify how long a contract binds the parties (e.g. 2 years, or until certain services are completed). Most terms in a contract are intended to expire once the term is complete. However, parties may occasionally want certain clauses to "survive" or still apply even after the contract term has expired. A survival clause sets forth those specific terms that need to live on after the contract expires or terminates. In a software development agreement, for example, the contract may terminate or expire once the software has been developed; however, the parties may want certain technical information used in the software development to remain confidential for many years after the contract expired. A survival clause (such as in Example 2) would accomplish this goal.

Third Party Beneficiary

Example 1: "No provision of this Agreement is intended to or shall create any rights in any third party with respect to the subject matter of this Agreement."

Example 2: "This Agreement is not intended to and shall not be construed to give any third party any interest or rights with respect to or in connection with any provision contained herein, except as otherwise expressly provided in this Agreement."

A contract usually exists between two parties that have signed a contract. These parties are said to be in "privity" because they are each bound by the terms of the contract. In contract law, the only parties that can enforce the terms of a contract, or file a lawsuit based on a contract, are generally the parties that are in privity of that contract. However, there are occasionally situations where a contract between Party A and Party B seems to give a third party, Party C, some benefit or obligation even though Party C is not a party to the contract. In such case, Party C may be able to enforce or file a lawsuit based on the contract between Party A and Party B as a "third party beneficiary" even though Party C never signed the contract. Third party beneficiary clauses address this and typically state the contract does *not* create any rights in any third parties. Where such clause exists, Party C would not be able to sue or enforce the terms of the contract between Party A and Party B. Third party beneficiary clauses can also be written to explicitly *give* a specific third party rights with respect to the contract, although that is less common than disclaiming any third party beneficiary. Ultimately, third party beneficiary clauses ensure that only intended parties are able to enforce the terms of a contract.

Venue

Example 1: "The Parties agree that the federal or state courts located in Minnesota shall have exclusive jurisdiction over the matters arising from or related to this Agreement."

Example 2: "Venue for any litigation shall be in any court of appropriate jurisdiction in Texas."

Venue clauses dictate the actual court in which a contract dispute would be heard and should not be confused with choice of law clauses. Venue can be defined very specifically (e.g. the United States District Court for the Southern District of New York), or generally (e.g. state courts in Florida). Venue and choice of law need not be the same, although they often are. Thus, it is theoretically possible to have venue in Texas, but governing law be the laws of Florida; in that case, a Texas court would apply Florida law with respect to interpreting an agreement. Venue clauses are important largely because they ensure convenience for a party – if you live in New York, you likely would want a venue clause to specify New York courts so you aren't dragged into court on the other side of the country.

Waiver

Example 1: "Waiver by either party of a breach of any provision of this Agreement shall not be construed as a waiver of any subsequent breach of the same or any other provision, nor shall any delay or omission on the part of such party to avail itself of any right, power or privilege that it has or may have hereunder operate as a waiver of any right, power or privilege."

Example 2: "No waiver of any provision of this Agreement shall be deemed valid unless signed in writing by both parties, nor will failure to enforce any right hereunder constitute a waiver of a provision of this Agreement or a waiver of any other right granted hereunder."

Waiver clauses ensure all terms of a contract remain enforceable, even if a party has not enforced the terms previously. Indeed, many contracts contain provisions that are always not enforced, but the parties want to be sure that unenforced provisions, and the rest of the contract, remain enforceable. This is important because there is a legal argument that if Party A fails to enforce a provision of a contract against

Party B, Party A has forfeited (i.e. waived) its right to enforce the term in the future. Where a waiver clause is used, such an argument becomes difficult or often impossible, to make.

I hope you have enjoyed this book and find it useful in your work or life. If you are a businessperson, you should have a greater confidence in your work, because boilerplate is no longer a foreign language to you. Likewise, if you merely want to have a better understanding of the contracts that surround you, this book should help you on your journey.

About the Author

Ethan Mobley is an entrepreneur and experienced transactional attorney. Ethan has significant experience drafting and negotiating commercial contracts while advising businesspeople on a wide range of legal issues. Much of Ethan's legal experience comes from working in-house for diverse companies in finance and technology. Outside of work, Ethan enjoys spending time with family, writing, and the exploring the outdoors.

Ethan holds a B.A. in Mathematical Sciences from Westminster College and a J.D. from the University of Minnesota Law School.